# VICTORIAN
## STRATFORD-UPON-AVON
## IN OLD PHOTOGRAPHS

FROM THE COLLECTIONS OF THE
SHAKESPEARE BIRTHPLACE TRUST

# VICTORIAN
## STRATFORD-UPON-AVON
# IN OLD PHOTOGRAPHS

### FROM THE COLLECTIONS OF THE
### SHAKESPEARE BIRTHPLACE TRUST

EDITED BY
# NICHOLAS FOGG

ALAN SUTTON

Alan Sutton Publishing Limited
Phoenix Mill · Far Thrupp · Stroud · Gloucestershire

First published 1990

**British Library Cataloguing in Publication Data**

Victorian Stratford-upon-Avon in old photographs.
1. Warwickshire. Stratford-upon-Avon, history
I. Fogg, Nicholas
942.489

ISBN 0-86299-831-X

Typeset in 9/10 Korinna.
Typesetting and origination by
Alan Sutton Publishing Limited.
Printed in Great Britain by
The Bath Press, Avon.

# CONTENTS

| | | |
|---|---|---:|
| | INTRODUCTION | 7 |
| 1. | A TOWN THAT SHAKESPEARE MIGHT HAVE RECOGNIZED | 9 |
| 2. | THE BIRTHPLACE RESTORED | 51 |
| 3. | CHURCH AND CHAPEL | 61 |
| 4. | EDUCATION | 75 |
| 5. | STRATFORD'S SATURNALIA | 85 |
| 6. | SOCIAL CHANGE | 95 |
| 7. | SHOTTERY | 109 |
| 8. | 'ABOUT THE BEST BEER BREWED IN ENGLAND' | 119 |
| 9. | 'EVERYTHING CONSPIRED TO MAKE THE OCCASION HAPPY' | 133 |
| 10. | 'SEND ME A GOOD FAST BOWLER TO PLAY LAERTES' | 145 |
| 11. | A NEW ERA | 155 |

VICTORIAN VALUES: cleanliness and civic pride. Statford's water supply is officially switched on by the mayor, Sir Arthur Hodgson, in 1886. This book delineates the transformation of the previously insanitary town during the Victorian era.

# INTRODUCTION

At the time of Queen Victoria's Diamond Jubilee in 1897, an elderly Stratfordian contrasted the town favourably with the town of his youth:

> It says something for the improvement in morals . . . that it is only necessary to pull down your blinds to shut up shop. There are no thieves and no burglars. The town . . . is well lighted; it has a fairly good trade, for I hardly ever see a shop to let, and it is impossible to get good houses. I think we might fairly consider ourselves to be in the happy position of being well managed.

The Chairman of the Magistrates made a similar comparison on the same occasion, 'The duties of the Bench are light and becoming lighter. People are becoming better and I think the schoolmaster has not been abroad to no purpose.'

This contrast between the beginning and the end of Victoria's reign is readily seen in contemporary photographic record. At the beginning of the era, we get a glimpse of a town that Shakespeare might, at least in part, have recognized – or, at least the place that the actor David Garrick, less than a century before, had described as 'the most dirty, unseemly, ill-paved, wretched-looking Town in all Britain.' Here is the Middle Row that once dissected Bridge Street; the old Guild House which had been inhabited by Shakespeare's cousin; the inn which occupied Shakespeare's birthplace during the poet's lifetime; the osier-beds along the Avon;

the coaches which once thundered through Stratford, changing their horses and discharging passengers at the great inns. Almost accidentally displayed are forgotten generations of Stratfordians, some born when North America was thirteen British colonies. Here is a world of tourism in its infancy. Shakespeare's birthplace is part of a domestic Grand Tour and the first movements towards a theatre have been achieved. We also see a forgotten industrial Stratford of busy wharves clustered around the canal basins, but, much to our loss, the camera is highly selective. We virtually lack any photographic record that tells us how our ancestors spent their working lives. There is no known picture of the local workhouse, which says much about contemporary social attitudes. Similarly the origins of the world-famous theatre which bears Shakespeare's name are restricted to the physical record of a building. No one considered a photographic record of the people who gave the building its importance.

The camera records the amazing process of change that characterized the Victorian Age – the coming of the railways, the arrival of sanitation and hygiene and, perhaps most crucially of all, the emergence of universal education. Most of the photographers are anonymous. One emerges as an outstanding artist: the Birmingham Member of Parliament, Sir Benjamin Stone. He alone recognized the necessity of recording an age which was passing. Without him vital events like the labourers plying for hire at the Mop and the children dancing in Benson's fantastical productions would remain mere verbal memories.

*Victorian Stratford in Old Photographs*, despite its limitations, represents a unique archive in the history of a place made all the more fascinating by the paradox that Stratford is both typical of the rest of England, yet made different by the Shakespearian connection. As the century progresses this gap widens and the Stratford of the tourist brochures becomes more apparent. Yet, beneath this gloss, an archetypal market town is still discernable.

Most of the pictures appear by courtesy of the Shakespeare Birthplace Trust. The movement which led to the acquisition of the Birthplace for the nation led also to the foundation of the Trust. Thus there has been a local history archive in Stratford for over a century, creating the most comprehensive local historical record in the country. I would like to thank Roger Pringle, Dr Robert Bearman, Maire Macdonald and Eileen Alberti from the Trust for their help and enthusiasm in the creation of this book – and Michael Coker, Director of Computing at Marlborough College for his continued tolerance and assistance.

# A Town that Shakespeare Might Have Recognized

*In 1832, one of the most exclusive schools for young ladies in England was Avonbank, which occupied St Mary's House by the Church gate at Stratford. The best known former pupil was Elizabeth Gaskell the novelist. Built as a medieval guildhouse, Thomas Greene, Town Clerk and 'cousin' to William Shakespeare, once lived there. . . .*

THE DUCHESS OF KENT visited Stratford in 1832, with her twelve-year-old daughter, Princess Victoria (later the queen).

IT WAS SUGGESTED THAT THE PRINCESS MIGHT ATTEND AVONBANK, however, nothing came of this. The house was demolished around 1864. The long entrance hall was known to the young ladies as 'the elephant's trunk' for obvious reasons.

WHILE IN STRATFORD Princess Victoria and her mother visited Shakespeare's birthplace which Thomas Court, a local publican, had bought from the Harts, descendents of Shakespeare's sister, in 1806. The inscription reads 'The Immortal Shakespeare was born in this house'. Note that the house was built as part of a terrace.

ADA COURT, widow of Thomas, seen here looking through the old serving hatch of the shop, entertained an increasing flow of visitors.

ONE OF THE HIGHLIGHTS of a visit to the birthplace was to inspect the names which celebrities (or pranksters on behalf of celebrities!) had inscribed on the windows (right) and walls (above right).

SHAKESPEARE'S BIRTHPLACE.

ONE SUCH VISITOR, in 1818, had been the celebrated American writer, Washington Irving. The room in which he stayed at the Red Horse was a further attraction for many years.

THE EASTERN HALF OF THE BIRTHPLACE had been converted into a tavern, the Swan and Maidenhead, in Shakespeare's day. It is curious to think of Shakespeare as the owner of a public house! It was popular with the drovers who brought their cattle into town on market days. The pub was pillaged by Parliamentary soldiers in 1643 and the orphan children of Jane Hiccox (Thomas and Anne) lost silver when Lord Brooke's forces came. A more jocular depredation occurred in 1808 when members of the Warwickshire Yeomanry pulled down the pub sign, declaring that 'as the only maidenhead left in Stratford was a wooden one, they would destroy it'.

THE PUB possessed its own brewhouse. The 'M' on the upper door may signify the malthouse where the barley would have been roasted.

THE FAME OF SHAKESPEARE brought an increasing number of visitors to the birthplace. The picture above was taken around 1845 and is probably the oldest known photograph taken in Stratford. Despite the poor quality of the image, two ladies may be seen arriving to pay homage at the literary shrine.

HOLY TRINITY CHURCH, where the poet is buried beneath his effigy (below, right), also attracted visitors. These pictures were taken around 1855.

THE COMIC ACTOR, CHARLES MATHEWS, in 1820, proposed that there should be a theatre in Stratford, 'A NATIONAL MONUMENT to the IMMORTAL MEMORY of SHAKESPEARE'. The Royal Shakespearian Theatre opened in New Place Gardens, once owned by the poet, in 1830. It was initially a great success. Edmund Kean played his celebrated Richard III there and W.C. McCready, Hamlet. After this, however, it went into decline and it was converted in 1844 into lecture rooms where occasional shows took place.

NEXT DOOR TO THE THEATRE WERE COTTAGES converted from a barn which is mentioned in Shakespeare's will. They were demolished in 1862.

ON THEIR VISIT in 1832, Princess Victoria and her mother stayed at the White Lion (above right), one of the most celebrated inns in England. Note the sign for the Swan and Maidenhead on the back wall of the Birthplace.

THE WHITE LION PROSPERED with the rise of coaching traffic but business waned with its decline and it closed in the late 1850s. Some local coach services continued throughout the Victorian Age. One is seen here outside the Red Horse.

THE MIDDLE ROW IN BRIDGE STREET. The buildings in the background were demolished around 1850, leaving the Swan Inn as the last building in this ancient block. It is possible that John Shakespeare, father of the poet, was apprenticed as a glovemaker to Alderman Thomas Dickson of the Swan. Both originated in the nearby village of Snitterfield. The inn was the scene of two murders in the early seventeenth century. In 1601 Thomas Bailes was 'slaine at the Signe of the Swan upon the sabbath day at the tyme of the sermon being there drinking'. In 1603, Lewis Gilbert, a veteran of the Irish wars, quarrelled with the host, Richard Waterman. When Waterman's brother, Thomas, attempted to eject him, Gilbert drew a long knife and stabbed him in the 'right side by the naval, from which he died'. Gilbert, of no fixed abode or means of support, fled.

THE SWAN (above) was demolished in 1863. The scholar, James Halliwell, declared that Robert Hobbes, who supervised the demolition, should 'in penance ... be made to stand in front of the Market House, looking at the waste he has created and have his ears lugged for his pains'. After its demolition the landlord, John Williams, who is probably pictured below, became a major in the US Army, serving on the frontier in the Indian wars.

ANOTHER NOTED STRATFORD HOSTELRY was the Shakespeare (above, around 1860), also known as Bolton's Commercial Inn after its proprietor.

AS WELL AS THE COACHING TRADE ALONG THE TURNPIKES, a network of carriers, which survived into this century, provided links with the surrounding district. This picture shows the van of Deacon and Burdett, the Bidford carriers at the turn of the century, near a local Victorian landmark, the Fountain.

A GREAT DEAL OF STABLING HAD TO BE PROVIDED in Stratford for both the coaching trade and carriers.

THE APPROACHES TO STRATFORD were very different then. There were no suburbs and the transition from country to town was immediate. Stratford was still virtually contained within its medieval boundaries. This Jacobean farmhouse, demolished in the 1930s to build a garage, stood on the junction of the Shipston and Banbury roads.

THESE MUD COTTAGES ON THE EVESHAM ROAD (above) were demolished before the Second World War.

THIS GEORGIAN LAMP PILLAR stood on the Warwick Road until the 1870s. The warehouses were also demolished around that time.

RURAL CRAFTS impinged within the borough boundary. This man is cutting osiers from a bed on the site of the present Theatre Gardens. They were used in basket making.

THE OSIER-BEDS photographed in about 1870.

OTHER OLD CRAFTS FLOURISHED. This whitetanners shop in the High Street, photographed around 1870, carried on the glovemaking trade once practised by William Shakespeare's father. The house, with its handsome carved frontage, was built in 1595 by Thomas Rogers. His grandson, John Harvard, was instrumental in founding the famous American university.

WHITE'S SADDLERS' SHOP at No. 13 Bridge Street, pictured in around 1890, served the extensive coaching and domestic trade.

BUSH'S, SHOEMAKERS AND COBBLERS, in Wood Street, a family business which flourished into this century, must also have used leather from local tanneries. The shop is pictured around 1860, before the innovation of plate glass windows changed the face of the town centre.

STRATFORD'S FIRST BANKS were opened in the early nineteenth century – this shows Lloyds Bank at the top of Bridge Street before its rebuilding in 1867.

THE INCREASED COACHING TRADE had necessitated, in 1814, the widening of the ancient bridge over the Avon, which had been built by Sir Hugh Clopton in the reign of Henry VII. This picture was taken in 1857. Note the toll-house, built in appropriate style, which reaped the revenues from this traffic.

HEAVIER GOODS WERE TRANSPORTED UP THE AVON, which had been navigable since 1634. The coming of the railway, in 1856, ensured that the navigation fell rapidly into disuse and disrepair. The picture above was taken around 1889.

THOMAS LUCY REBUILT THE OLD MILL by the church in 1819, reputedly using money from a settlement on the family estate at Charlecote. He shipped corn up the river after 1830 in a steam barge.

THE PICTURE ABOVE WAS TAKEN FROM CROSS O' THE HILL before the coming of the railway in 1855. Lucy's Mill can be seen in front of the church. Note the Mill Bridge and the old drovers' track in the foreground.

THE AVON NAVIGATION WAS EXTENDED in 1816, when the Stratford Canal opened, providing a link with the Grand Union. Soon 48,000 tons of coal were being shipped through Stratford annually, the barges discharging their cargoes at basins on the Bancroft. Wharves were established along the canalside.

NUMEROUS BUSINESSES WERE ESTABLISHED. These were the premises of Scott and Company, lead and glass merchants, on the Bancroft, where the Gower Memorial now stands. The picture was taken about 1890.

THIS WAS A TIME OF GREAT DISAFFECTION. Rural poverty led to acts of arson. The fire–engine was frequently called out from its shed in what had once been the Guild Hall to fires on nearby farms.

EDWARD FORDHAM FLOWER AND JAMES COX, in 1827, founded a timber merchant's buiness on the wharves behind the One Elm. Cox was a devout Christian and, like Flower, an earnest social reformer. In 1832, he opened a 'ragged school' in Sheep Street for forty poor children. The street is seen above around 1860. Note the Green Man on the left and the Dog on the right, two of Stratford's vanished pubs.

COX AND FLOWER DIVIDED THEIR BUSINESS in 1832 and Flower opened a brewery on the site. The picture shows workers (and some of their dogs) outside the old brewery around 1899.

COX PROVIDED COOPERAGE FROM HIS TIMBERYARD next to Clopton Bridge. The large tree trunks (below) have been brought up river by barge and lifted on to the quay by the crane prior to going through the saw-mill – about 1865.

NEARBY WAS THE NEW BRIDGE which, since 1826, had carried the Grand Junction Railway to Moreton-in-Marsh, part of a grand design never fulfilled, to link Stratford's waterways to London. Despite George Stephenson recommending steampower, the engineer, William James, preferred the certainties of horse locomotion. Thus the enterprise rapidly became a 'superceded idea', although the tramway did not close until 1875. The last surviving wagon, clearly adapted from farm use, remains on the last section of rail at the end of the bridge.

THE TRAMWAY in the 1870s. It ran parallel with the Shipston Road. The flange-rails were removed in 1918.

FURTHER PROGRESS CAME in 1834, when Stratford Gasworks opened in Chapel Lane. The premises are now the Union Club.

THE FIRST GAS COOKER IN STRATFORD was installed at the Falcon Inn, seen here around 1860. 'For cleanliness, cheapness and saving of trouble, nothing could surpass it.'

BECAUSE THE COST OF GAS WAS HIGH, there were few street lights. One of the earliest stood on the corner of Scholar's Lane. It contrasts with the old 'lanthorn' on the nearby house. Burgesses were obliged, before the arrival of street lighting, to provide lights of this type on their houses.

EDWARD FLOWER was elected to Stratford Corporation in 1836. Meetings were held in the Town Hall, pictured above around 1880. The Corn Exchange is on the left.

THIS WAS A TIME OF GREAT CONTROVERSY. The Borough had established a four-man police force, to 'strut about the streets insinuating that the people are becoming thieves and pickpockets'. The constable on the left is pictured around 1847.

MAYOR AT THIS TIME WAS ALDERMAN DAVID RICE, a surgeon, depicted here shortly before his death in 1860. He was born in 1799. He made himself unpopular by ordering the sequestration of goods of shopkeepers who infringed the by-laws on Sunday opening – the only time when many working people could shop.

HIS WIFE, MARY, whom he married in 1829, came from a noted local family, the Hobbes. She was born in 1805. Her father was Town Clerk in 1818.

APART FROM HOBBES, the Town Clerks came from the Hunt family for over a century, the descendants of Thomas Hunt who was instrumental in David Garrick's famous Shakespeare Jubilee of 1769. Pictured left is William Oakes Hunt, Town Clerk in the 1870s.

ANOTHER CONTROVERSY INVOLVED THE CHURCH. All parishioners were liable for a Church Rate. Nonconformists objected to contributing to the upkeep of a church which they did not attend and frequently refused to pay. Among those locally who had goods distrained for non-payment were James Cox and the Independent minister, the Revd Thomas Helmore.

THE CORPORATION HAD RESPONSIBILITY FOR THE TOWN'S ANCIENT GRAMMAR SCHOOL, which occupied part of the Medieval Guild buildings. It was here that William Shakespeare was educated. The school traces its origins to an endowment by Thomas Joliffe, a priest of the Guild, in 1427 but undoubtedly goes back further than this. In the 1830s, although there were seldom more than fifteen pupils, the master received the handsome annual salary of £145. In 1837, the matter was raised in Parliament and both the curriculum and the size of the intake were reformed. Yet the school remained little more than a superior elementary school. In 1869 it contained fifty-two boys (five of whom boarded). Only in 1880 was a discretionary scholarship established to enable boys to come from local primary schools.

THE BOYS WERE TAUGHT IN THE ORIGINAL SCHOOLROOM, which dates from the endowment. It is the oldest schoolroom still in use in England. The desks on the far side of the room date from the eighteenth century.

THE MASTER'S SALARY included £30 in lieu of the house (left), which was considered insufficiently grand for him and became dilapidated.

THE REFORM PROVIDED MORE OPPORTUNITY for the sons of rising middle-class families like that of David Plumb, who was trading as an ironmonger at No. 40 High Street in 1851. The picture was taken around 1857, after the family had moved to Weston-super-Mare.

ANOTHER OF THE CORPORATION'S RESPONSIBILITIES was for its medieval almshouses, next to the Grammar School, founded by the Guild of the Holy Cross in 1269.

A PENSIONER in 1899: an interesting survival who still wears an embroidered smock – once the standard costume for a working man. This picture and the one opposite, below, were taken by Benjamin Stone.

STRATFORD WAS CHANGING RAPIDLY. Older inhabitants could reflect on a popular local song, 'They won't let any of our old things be'. Miss Anne Wheler, pictured left and above in her garden at Old Town Croft in the 1850s, was the daughter of Francis Wheler, the Recorder of Stratford, who had proposed the Jubilee of 1769 to David Garrick. Her brother, Robert Bell Wheler, wrote the first *History of Stratford* in 1806.

AN INQUIRY BY THE BOARD OF HEALTH in 1848 revealed the insanitary and primitive state of Stratford. In wet weather the unmetalled roads were deep in mud and scarcely passable for vehicles. Each householder paved as he chose in front of his house. Many favoured a cheap flagstone, known locally as 'petrified kidneys', which split easily, forming muddy puddles. The pictures above shows Old Town around 1855.

THE INSPECTOR APPOINTED BY THE BOARD declared that he had never visited a place where the link between 'damp and dirt and sickness and increased expenditure has been so clearly established'. There was no house drainage and few water closets. The chief water supply was from pumps, frequently situated near cess pits. This pump stood at the top of Bridge Street.

OTHER INHABITANTS used the canal as a water supply. Although it was very dirty, the water was softer than that from the river, which was hardly ever used. The picture, taken by Benjamin Stone in 1899, shows women fetching water from Shottery Brook – Anne Hathaway's Cottage may be seen in the background. The inhabitants of Shottery continued to obtain water by traditional methods long after other Stratfordians had secured pure supplies.

MOST BURIALS WERE IN THE CRAMPED PARISH CHURCHYARD. The vicar considered that if there were a severe epidemic, it would be difficult to find plots without encroaching on newly dug graves. A national typhoid epidemic occurred in 1848, but there was only an isolated case in Stratford.

STRATFORD WAS DIVIDED between those who wanted the Board of Health's report implemented, who included Edward Flower and Charles Lucy, and the 'economists', who were cautious about costs. The parties coalesced around public houses. The Falcon was in favour of increasing spending, while the Seven Stars (right) supported the economists.

DESPITE OPPOSITION, a local Board of Health was established in 1850. Sappers and miners of the Royal Engineers surveyed the lines of drains and sewers, using the tower of the Guild Chapel as a vantage point.

WORK PROCEEDED SLOWLY. The picture above shows excavation of the sewers in Bridge Street around 1855 – the last pipe was laid in 1859.

THE MAIN STREETS WERE METALLED. The picture shows a horse-drawn roller in Union Street around 1860.

OUTSIDERS BEGAN TO COMMENT FAVOURABLY ON THE TOWN. The streets, it was reported by the *Athenaum*, had been made 'to gleam so bright and smell so sweet'. Compare the picture above – the neat pavements and metalled road of the High Street with those of earlier days.

YET, THE *ATHENAUM* WRITER HAD NOT WANDERED FAR. Most streets remained unpaved. The new sanitation was barely adequate and wretched housing remained the lot of many. The picture above shows Garrick Court in the 1890s: one of Stratford's old alleys later demolished to build the Picture House. Note the bird cages on the walls of the cottages.

THE INSPECTOR proposed that a cattle-market should be established, thus removing a considerable amount of animal excrement from the streets. This was not done for twenty years, however. The cattle-market, pictured here in 1899, is still on its original site by the railway station.

SECTION TWO

# The Birthplace Restored

*Even in the early nineteenth century, the economic importance of tourism to Stratford was considerable. The town had lost its woollen trade and, as the* Monthly Magazine *commented in 1818, 'having no manufactory would be one of the begging places of of the Kingdom – but for the renown of Shakespeare, and the numerous visitors drawn to the place'. One of the major attractions was a collection of spurious Shakespearian relics assembled by Mary Hornby, who was tenant of the birthplace until she was evicted by Ada Court, who was jealous of her growing commercial success. Mrs Hornby moved her relics to premises across the street and the two dowagers would stand on their respective doorsteps to abuse each other – and anyone entering the rival premises. A wag was moved to verse:*

> *What – Birthplace here – and relics there!*
> *Abuse from each! Ye brawling blowses! –*
> *Each picks my pocket – 'tis not fair –*
> *A stranger's curse on both your houses!*

*On the death of Mrs Hornby, her daughter-in-law maintained this great attraction in new premises near the Town Hall.*

MRS COURT died in 1846 and the Shakespeare birthplace was put up for auction. Wild rumours circulated. It was said that Phineas T. Barnum, the American showman, wanted to ship the property brick-by-brick, across the Atlantic.

A SHAKESPEARE'S BIRTHPLACE COM-MITTEE WAS FORMED under the patronage of Queen Victoria and Prince Albert.

MANY AND VARIOUS WERE THE FUND-
RAISING ACTIVITIES of the Shake-
speare's Birthplace Committee.
The celebrated soprano, Jenny
Lind, sang and Charles Dickens
organized theatricals.

SHAKESPEARE'S BIRTHPLACE was sold
to the united committees of Stratford and London on 16 September
1847. The auctioneer, pictured
above, was Mr Edmund Robbins.

IT WAS DECREED that Shakespeare's house, always part of a terrace, should stand alone, so those of his neighbours were pulled down.

THE AGE DEMANDED A PICTURESQUE GARDEN, so down came the barns, outhouses, piggeries and brewhouse, reminders of the working life which was the property's *raison d'etre*. The White Lion can be seen in the background.

IT WAS RESOLVED TO RESTORE THE BIRTHPLACE to its original condition. The problem was that no one knew how this decaying pile of bricks had looked in Shakespeare's day. Folk memories of a large gable were confirmed by a drawing, made a century before. In the absence of anything better, the building was restored to conform to that impression. The original massive beams interfered with the 'fanciful composition' of the architect, Alderman Edward Gibbs, so they were pulled down. The restored birthplace was described by a critic as 'a spick and span new villa, standing in its own grounds'. This picture was taken around 1857 by Edward Adams, who, three years later, founded the *Stratford-upon-Avon Herald*.

THE FLOW OF VISITORS TO THE BIRTHPLACE was increased by the coming of the railways in 1859. The main station linked the lines of the Stratford Railway Company from Hatton and the Oxford, Worcester and Wolverhampton Company from Honeybourne. Both were absorbed into the Great Western Railway in 1883. The picture above shows station staff around 1898.

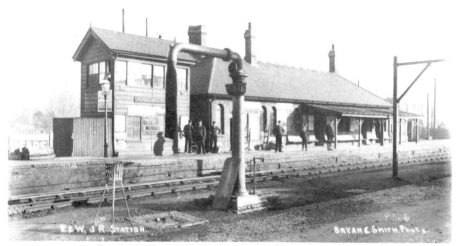

A SECOND LINE, the East and West Junction Railway, provided another link with the national network. The station, seen above, was in New Street.

A TRAIN LEAVING THE NEW STREET STATION in 1896. Lucy's Mill is in the background.

THE RED HORSE HOTEL took advantage of the railway to establish a station bus for its customers which could run on rail or road. The picture here shows it in about 1890. The 'Ro-railer' was a feature of town life until the 1930s.

THEY CAME FROM ALL OVER THE WORLD. These wives of Maori chiefs were among the 6,000 visitors to the birthplace in 1863.

THE BIRTHPLACE TRUST acquired the site of New Place, Shakespeare's last home, in 1864, pictured here around 1855, and the adjacent Nash's House, with its Georgian frontage. On the left is Stratford's Fire Office.

NASH'S HOUSE was restored, with the same comprehensive approach that had prevailed at the birthplace, in 1911. The site of New Place is behind the wall on the left. The building work revealed the original line of the gables on the side of Nash's House.

VISITORS FREQUENTLY COMMENTED on the way Stratfordians spoke of Shakespeare as if he were still alive and their eagerness to tell stories about him.

THE RAILWAY ALSO BROUGHT A HUGE INFLUX OF DAY-TRIPPERS to the town, mainly from local industrial areas like Birmingham. The picture above shows some of them at the Mill Bridge around 1906.

# Church and Chapel

On Sunday, 30 March, 1851, a unique religious census took place nationally. As part of this, Ministers of Religion made returns on attendance at the eight places of worship. Although the method of assessment was crude, the survey gives an indication of the state of religion in the town.

The results of the survey shocked churchmen – both locally and nationally. Although the attendance levels were very high, it was revealed that there was an entire class of people who never, or rarely, attended. These were mainly drawn from the poorest stratas of society. When non-attenders in Stratford were asked why they did not go to church, they replied that it was too far, or the services were too long, or the free seats were no good. Thus an impetus to home evangelism was born. The building of St James' church was part of this process.

AT HOLY TRINITY there were 800 worshippers at Morning Service and 900 at Evensong. The Morning Sunday school was attended by 160 children with 100 in the evening.

THE GUILD CHAPEL was in the charge of its own priest-chaplain appointed by the Corporation. There were frequent disputes with the vicar about jurisdiction. The seventy-five free sittings were always occupied and there were constant applications for the 276 seats that were let. Note the gas mantles on the walls in this picture.

THE ONLY OTHER ANGLICAN CHURCH IN THE PARISH was St Peter's at Bishopton. On Census Sunday, Evensong – generally conducted by one of the curates of Holy Trinity – was attended by fifty-five people.

ST JAMES' CHURCH was consecrated in the Guild Pits in 1855, 'to serve that class of persons whom it is eminently desirable to draw within the fold of the Church.' The new church never really succeeded in establishing a strong base. It was demolished in the 1950s.

THE INDEPENDENT (OR CONGREGATIONAL) CHAPEL in Rother Street was built in a spirit of optimism about the demise of the established Church. Although it had a capacity of 700, on Census Sunday 126 worshippers attended in the morning and 210 in the evening, with 133 children in the Sunday school. Next door to the chapel is Mason's Court, one of Stratford's finest medieval buildings. The Independents built the new chapel on the right of the picture in 1880. The old chapel became a working mens' club. It was demolished in 1964.

THE WESLEYAN METHODIST MEETING IN STRATFORD began in 1819. In 1866, this chapel was built on the Birmingham Road. On Census Sunday, there were 80 worshippers in the morning, 50 in the afternoon and 120 in the evening.

THE PRIMITIVE METHODISTS first met in a converted barn (left) behind Shakespeare's birthplace in 1832.

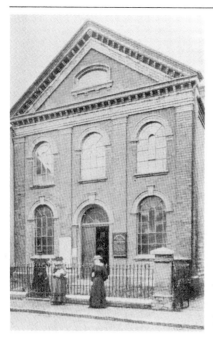

THE PRIMITIVE METHODISTS consecrated this chapel in Great William Street in 1866. It closed in 1932 after a re-amalgamation with the Wesleyans. The building is now a Masonic Lodge.

JOSEPH ARCH, a local hedger, was a Primitive Methodist lay preacher. In 1872, he formed the Warwickshire Labourers' Union, the first such body. He frequently addressed meetings in the Rother Market during the subsequent farmworkers' strike. In 1885 he became Liberal MP for North-West Norfolk and, in 1893, the first working-man to serve in the Cabinet.

THE ELEGANT PARTICULAR BAPTIST CHAPEL was built by James Cox, the timber merchant, in 1835. On Census Sunday there were 100 worshippers in the morning and 120 in the evening, with 120 children in Sunday school.

BIBLICAL STUDY was a feature of the Nonconformist churches. The picture above shows the Baptist Ladies' Bible Class, run by the obviously formidable Miss Lee (centre) around 1880.

ALL THE DENOMINATIONS RAN SUNDAY SCHOOLS. The picture above probably shows a Sunday school outing of indeterminate allegiance about to depart from Greenhill Street around 1908.

WORSHIP WAS COMPULSORY AT THE WORKHOUSE on Arden Street. Morning service was attended by 62 paupers and 59 in the evening. It reveals much of contemporary social attitudes that this is the only public building in Stratford with no known surviving photograph. In 1899, Benjamin Stone photographed this man, probably a stonemason, outside the church. Let him symbolize all those working people for whom the workhouse was an ever-present shadow.

JAMES COX JUN., a genial, liberal-minded man, who did much to enhance the local prestige of the Roman Catholic Church.

THERE WAS NO CATHOLIC CHURCH in Stratford at this time. The forty or so local Catholics were ministered to by Benedictines from Wootton Wawen. After two attempts to find premises had collapsed, a church was erected on the Warwick Road, based on designs by the celebrated architect, Augustus Pugin. It was consecrated in 1866. The handsome little building was built largely through the largesse of James Cox, jun., son of the Baptist benefactor, who was a convert to Catholicism. The track to the left of the church became the Welcombe Road. On the right is the Warwick Road.

THE REVD GEORGE GRANVILLE, who became vicar in 1854, judiciously defused the issue of Church Rates (see p. 39) by declaring his personal opposition, while defending the right of the churchwardens to levy them.

SOME PEOPLE WERE DEEPLY SUSPICIOUS of Anglo-Catholic tendencies discernable at Holy Trinity. Such modest innovations as candles, flowers and a cross on the altar were condemned by the Archdiaconal visitation in 1860.

HOLY TRINITY was beautified by the eminent architect, William Butterfield, in 1854. At the reconsecration service, the congregation were amazed by a procession of surpliced choristers. The sub-vicar explained the changes and declared that they were 'as far away as ever from the Roman Church'. The picture, taken around 1899, shows the choir with the then vicar, George Arbuthnot. By then parishioners had got used to what had once been regarded as dangerous innovations. The choir had been founded in the 1830s. Its most celebrated choirmaster was Thomas Helmore, son of the Independent minister and a great influence in the revival of church music. His best known arrangement is the great Advent carol 'O Come, O Come, Emmanuel'.

FURTHER EXTENSIVE RESTORATION took place in 1890. The picture shows work on the spire.

GRANVILLE'S SUCCESSOR AS VICAR in 1867 was Dr John Day Collis, another Anglo-Catholic and a great social reformer. Many of his achievements had a lasting effect. He founded the National Burial Reform Committee to campaign for an end to the tradition of elaborate and expensive funerals which was an enormous burden for the poor.

DR COLLIS founded a parochial organization for the sick poor under the charge of Miss Emily Minet, who had trained with Florence Nightingale. The result of their work was the local Childrens' Recovery Hospital. Miss Minet organized a soup kitchen at the Town Hall to alleviate hardship among the poor during bad weather when seasonal unemployment could reach twenty per cent. Each year she (and her successors) launched an appeal for funds. The picture above shows an ox-roast on the frozen river to raise money in 1895 – one of a series of severe winters in the late Victorian era.

GEORGE ARBUTHNOT, who succeeded Dr Collis in 1879, continued the traditions of social Catholicism. He was a powerful force behind the building of a general hospital (below) in 1885. The hospital had its origins in a dispensary for the sick poor founded in Chapel Street in 1824 by a local doctor, John Conolly, who later became one of the great reformers in the treatment of mental illness.

# SECTION FOUR

# Education

*Education was a great battlefield between the denominations; the only public education available for much of Victoria's reign was that provided by the churches. The Church of England's National School was founded around 1810 and moved to premises on the Alcester Road in 1844.*

*As befits a former pupil of Dr Arnold, Dr Collis had a great interest in education. In 1868, he acquired Mason's Croft, an old town house in Church Street. After adding a storey, he opened the building as a boys' independent school, Trinity College. He gathered a group of able teachers and soon the school was attended by pupils from all over the country.*

*After the death of Dr Collis in 18–, the school's reputation declined. In 1908 it moved to Maidenhead and was renamed the Royal Army School.*

MASON'S CROFT around 1865.

TRINITY COLLEGE around 1875. Note the additional storey.

THE STAFF OF TRINITY COLLEGE pictured around 1880.

THE NEW SCHOOL was a threat to Stratford's old grammar school, which still had less than forty pupils. Its fortunes improved rapidly under the headmastership of the Revd R. de Courcy Laffan, an early supporter of women's suffrage, who expanded the curriculum and introduced organized games. When he departed to become headmaster of Cheltenham College a decade later, there were over one hundred pupils.

WHILE DR LAFFAN WAS HEADMASTER the grammar school's ancient buildings were restored, in 1893, through the generosity of the wealthy brewer, Charles Flower. The neighbouring Guild Chapel was restored at the same time. The picture below shows workmen on the site. Has the woman brought someone's lunch?

MRS LAFFAN, A WELL-KNOWN ROMANTIC NOVELIST, revived the charming custom, begun by Dr Collis, of the boys of Shakespeare's school processing to the church on his birthday and laying flowers on his grave.

THE VICAR invited 'great and small' to do the same and began a continuing tradition in 1899.

THE SECOND BIRTHDAY PROCESSION passing Avoncroft in 1900. The mayor seems to have been sidefooted on to the pavement. The celebration expanded rapidly. By the First World War it included the unfurling of the flags of the nations in Bridge Street, the procession, a luncheon and a special theatre performance.

FOR MOST LEARNING WAS RESTRICTED TO BASIC LITERACY. The picture above shows the small boys of the National (C of E) School in the 1890s.

THE BRITISH SCHOOL was favoured by the Nonconformists. It was founded by the Independent minister, the Revd Thomas Helmore, around 1815. The first schoolmaster was William Pardoe, seen here shortly before his death in 1860.

PRIMARY EDUCATION BECAME COMPULSORY in 1878. The obligation to improve school buildings led to the closure of the British School in 1881. Because the National School was unable to adequately provide education for all the children of Stratford, the town was legally obliged to elect a School Board in 1881, which was responsible for the new Board School in Broad Street, which opened in 1883, under the auspices of the Department of Education. The picture above, beautifully posed by Benjamin Stone, shows a class of girls – the sexes were segregated – at Broad Street School in 1899. Note their neat aprons.

AT FIRST THE SCHOOL BOARD WAS DOMINATED BY THE CHURCH PARTY led by the vicar, the Revd George Arbuthnot. School Board elections were stormy affairs, usually reflecting the strength of the various denominations. They ceased in 1902, when the powers of the School Board passed to the newly-formed Warwickshire Education Committee. The picture above, again beautifully posed by Benjamin Stone, shows a class of Broad Street boys. Note the uniformly worn collars, boots, breeches, waistcoats and jackets.

TWO INFANT CLASSES in around 1899. The reception class (above) was mixed. Some of the children were very young. It would appear from the faces that the photographer has kept everybody waiting. Note the pretty teacher on the right. The older girl on the right below was probably a pupil-teacher, employed to help with the junior classes in return for extra lessons.

# Stratford's Saturnalia

*Despite differences over education, temperance was an area of cooperation between the churches: Stratford had its own branch of the inter-denominational Temperance League, which campaigned for more restrictive licensing laws.*

*Another area of common-cause was 'the great work of moral purification'. A Vigilance Association was formed 'for the repression of vice and public immorality'. There were a number of houses of ill-fame in Victorian Stratford. When, in 1891, the police noted the names of visitors to a brothel in Meer Street, it was pleaded that many were in 'respectable positions' and several were married. The Ship Inn on Waterside was notorious. In 1869, a paternity suit was dismissed because the plaintiff had been seen there.*

*Another spectacle which drew moral fire was the Mop Fair on 12 October, described by the* Herald *as 'Stratford's Saturnalia' and its smaller counterpart, the Runaway Mop on the following Friday week. Attempts to abolish the fair were firmly resisted, the* Herald *criticising those who sought to take from the poor man the 'last remaining holiday which grasping avarice has left him'.*

THE FOUNTAIN TEMPERANCE HOTEL in Rother Street was a practical expression of the aims of the Temperance League.

WATERSIDE IN THE FLOODS. The notorious Ship stands on the far right. Note the warehouses opposite.

ONE OF THE CAUSES OF DISTASTE was the reason for the Mop's original existence – the system whereby labourers and servants plied for hire in the streets. Pictured here are three such labourers, each with the symbol of his trade in his buttonhole. The name of the fair probably originates with the strands of mop worn by maidservants plying for hire. It was suggested that the system could be used to procure girls for prostitution. This led to the foundation of a Servants' Amelioration Society – the forerunner of Labour Exchanges. The hiring system gradually declined, although it survived until the First World War.

CRITICS OF THE FAIR claimed that once hiring was accomplished and a gratuity gained, the rest of the day was spent in 'immoral amusements which bring degradation on many a young female and sorrow to many an honest parent'. The picture below shows Chipperfield's showgirls attracting the crowds in Bridge Street.

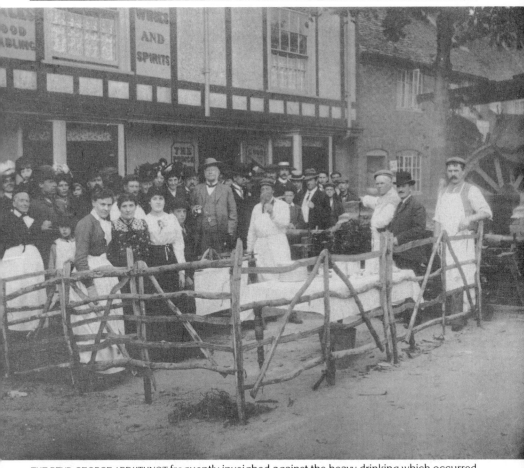

THE REVD GEORGE ARBUTHNOT frequently inveighed against the heavy drinking which occurred on Mop Day. The Mop was famous for its roasts which were established outside pubs. At the Prince of Wales in Rother Street, now the offices of the Stratford *Herald*, a celebrated roaster 'Judy' Hewins, operated for over fifty years. The inn was kept by the Goodman family, who may be seen in the left foreground. The distinguished-looking gentleman wearing the hat in the middle is Sir Arthur Hodgson of Clopton House. 'Judy' Hewins was the grandfather of George Hewins, hero of a much loved local book, *The Dillen*. George recalled stuffing his pockets with stale crusts and catching the dripping as his grandfather carved.

ANOTHER CELEBRATED ROASTER was 'Panham' Worrall, here presiding at the Garrick.

NEARLY EVERY PUB HAD ITS ROAST. Pictured here are those at the White Swan . . .

AND THE SEVEN STARS.

STEAM ENGINES had largely taken over from manual and animal traction by the 1890s. The one here is depicted driving the galloping horses in Rother Street. Another ox-roast is in the foreground.

THIS WAS SURELY THE MOP'S HEYDAY, as 'big shows' brought all the fun of the fair.

WHILE THE MOP FLOURISHED, other old customs were dying out. The last official swan upping on the River Avon took place around 1886. The ceremony was designed to count the swans and mark them for their owners. It ended in a traditional feast. Among the dignatories taking part here was Superintendent Thomas Rowley, who was in charge of the Stratford Police Force. He is seated on the right in the boat nearest the river bank. The meadow behind is the modern recreation ground.

# SECTION SIX

# Social Change

*For all the excitement generated by the Mop, Stratford was generally a tranquil place. The* Herald *regarded bicycles, velocipedes and perambulators as being the main hazards to a peaceful existence.*

*In the 1960s, Miss F.D. Rowley, whose father was Police Superintendent, remembered the main excitement as being on market days when breeders showed their horses in the streets. This practice ceased in 1892 after complaints about 'indecent exhibitions'. A groom was prosecuted for exposing a stallion to show.*

'BICYCLES, VELOCIPEDES AND PERAMBULATORS... the main hazards to a peaceful existence.'
Henley Street in the 1890s.

HORSES WERE TETHERED FOR DISPLAY, much to the scandal of local moralists, at rings like these on a wall in Rother Street.

OTHER DIVERSIONS included an occasional visit from a brass band. The one here visited Stratford around 1867. Many such bands came from Germany and played outside local pubs. Despite the disapproval of the temperance movement, the pubs were great social centres. The picture overleaf (top) shows the excursion organized by the Swan's Nest in Bridgetown in 1890. Originally known as the Shoulder of Mutton, it was kept by the Rose family as a common lodging house, but became a smart inn at around this time. The family still run the nearby boathouse on the Avon.

EXCURSION FROM THE SWAN'S NEST.

ROYAL OCCASIONS WERE WELL CELEBRATED. On the Diamond Jubilee of Queen Victoria, Stratfordians dined in Bridge Street.

TO COMMEMORATE THE SAME OCCASION, a wealthy Philadelphian, George W. Childs, gave the American Fountain in Rother Street. The ceremony is pictured above. The Fountain may be seen on p. 22. The unveiling was performed by the famous actor, Henry Irving (below), one of the few 'greats' never to appear at the Stratford theatre. He was due to do so in 1905, but withdrew because of illness which turned out to be terminal. The Fountain became a popular venue for public meetings in the era before the First World War.

ANOTHER ROYAL OCCASION above: the gathering in 1895 to celebrate the wedding of Duke and Duchess of York, later King George V and Queen Mary. Social change was bringing demands for better working conditions and increased leisure, but times were still hard for many workers. The picture above right shows the employees of R.M. Bird's mineral water plant in 1895. In 1873, a public meeting at the Town Hall demanded an early closing day and the adoption of Bank Holidays for shopworkers. The shopkeepers agreed provided that all did it, but Fred Winter refused to close his drapers' shop. James Cox jun. expressed the strong public sympathy for the shop assistants when he proposed a boycott of Winter's business: 'If the ladies will only help us, it can be done'.

EVENTUALLY, WINTER AGREED TO CLOSE TWO HOURS EARLIER – at 5 p.m. – on Wednesdays. His shop, pictured around 1900, can be seen under the awning in the picture below.

ALL THE LOCAL SHOPS WERE FAMILY BUSINESSES. Meadows, grocers and tea dealers at No. 30 High Street, are pictured left in around 1870.

A SMALL CORNER SHOP occupied this ancient building in Ely Street. It was once the home of John Jordan, the 'wheelwright poet' who had invented many legends about Shakespeare in the previous century. The building was demolished by civic vandals in the 1960s.

FRIDAY WAS MARKET DAY and the stalls occupied the middle of Bridge Street from the Market House, the domed building at the top (now Barclays Bank).

PEARCE'S DINING ROOMS were in Wood Street for a number of years. The proprietor, Mr N. Pearce, is seen left, on his doorstep. The family ran catering businesses in Stratford until the 1950s.

THE NEW POST OFFICE IN SHEEP STREET which has since been demolished. Public protest saved the old house on the left from civic vandals in the 1960s.

A NEW FORM OF SHOPPING came in the 1890s with the opening of the Co-op, also in Sheep Street. The staff look exceptionally smart.

A SATURDAY HALF-HOLIDAY WAS BECOMING GENERAL and football the passion of the masses. In 1873 Stratford played Birmingham in the first local match – the all-absorbing topic with local fans. Stratford lost, but played well. The Rugby Club was formed at about this time and from its earliest days played on Pearcecroft, south of the river. The Cricket Club had been formed earlier in Victoria's reign. Quieter forms of recreation included boating, which was particularly popular with visitors to Stratford. The picture shows one of the local boathouses in Southern Lane by the ferry. On the opposite bank is the newly-acquired Recreation Ground, which soon catered for a variety of sports. A new form of recreation came to Stratford in 1896 with the arrival of the first motor cars. Their ugliness, lack of comfort and smell were much remarked upon. Only recently had the necessity for them to be preceded by a man with a red flag been abolished.

THE BOAT CLUB, founded in 1874, became one of the most successful in the Midlands. The clubhouse was built in the mock-Tudor style thought appropriate to Shakespeare's town.

AVONDALE ROVERS, pictured here around 1900: an early local football team.

OTHERS FAVOURED 'THE OVAL CODE'. Stratford rugby team in the 1870s.

ARCHIE FLOWER (LATER SIR ARCHIE), who was to become Chairman of the Brewery and the Theatre Governers, captained the side in 1889–90.

WOMEN, TOO, WERE ENJOYING NEW PASTIMES: lady cyclists outside the birthplace in 1896.

AN EARLY RILEY CAR taking part in a commemoration run in around 1924. Note the man with the red flag.

# SECTION SEVEN

# Shottery

*Stratford was surrounded by contiguous villages and hamlets which, into the late Victorian Age, preserved vestiges of a vanishing rural way of life – a changelessness that was grounded in poverty. Shottery was the best-known of these. It was a long, sprawling village which possessed neither a church nor a schoolbuilding for much of Victoria's reign. Occasional services were held in a tithe barn and the eighty village children were educated in the cramped surroundings of a Congregational Chapel. The energies of that ubiquitous vicar, Dr Collis, were not confined to Stratford, however. He ensured that Shottery should have both a church and a school. The centres of the local community were the little village post office and the Shakespeare Tavern. Fighting was a major pastime. After the tavern closed, the young men of the village would often form a ring and wrestle for each other's belts – a practice eventually stopped by the police.*

THE MAIN STREET IN SHOTTERY. Note the Temperance Hotel on the left.

SHOTTERY POST OFFICE in 1884. The proprietress was Miss Sarah Webster Hunt.

THE VILLAGE CULMINATED IN A DIRT ROAD that led to a group of primitive and picturesque cottages, known as 'The Barracks'. They were later renamed 'Hathaway Hamlet' in response to the growing tourist industry. This remarkable picture shows a group of women gossiping there in 1892.

SHOTTERY'S CHURCH OF ST ANDREW was consecrated in 1870.

THE ENDOWMENT CAME LARGELY FROM ADMIRAL CURRY, tenant of Shottery Hall.

SHOTTERY SCHOOL moved into the more spacious quarters of a converted tithe barn in 1870. The barn was transported from Redditch.

A LANTERN SLIDE OF LOCAL SCHOOLCHILDREN outside Anne Hathaway's Cottage in 1896.

ANNE HATHAWAY'S COTTAGE, pictured here around 1858, brought an increasing flow of visitors to Shottery. One of them may be seen on the step, wearing a stovepipe hat. The house was originally called 'Hewland's Farm', but the name was changed to reflect the fact that it was the girlhood home of Shakespeare's wife. Note the name-plate on the wall and what are probably privies in front of the house on the right. They were removed in the 1870s, probably in response to the necessity of making the house as picturesque as possible for the tourists. The dirt track in the foreground leads to the Barracks. The picture above right, taken about 1860, probably shows some of the last generation of the family to live there. The path in front of the cottage was a public right of way.

THE HATHAWAYS lived at the property for over 400 years. The last lineal descendent to inhabit the building was Mrs Mary Baker, seen below, seated. The other people may be her relatives.

LIKE THE OWNERS OF THE BIRTHPLACE, the Hathaways had always sought to exploit their ancestral good fortune, selling, in 1793, the chair 'on which Shakespeare had sat with Anne on his knee'. In 1830, a local directory revealed that the cottage had been provided, some years before, with several pieces of furniture 'affirmed to have belonged to the poet', including his 'courting chair'.

MRS BAKER DELIGHTED IN SHOWING VISITORS THE HOUSE and was a noted local character. She is pictured above with her family Bible on the table next to her.

MRS BAKER IN THE GARDEN with a visitor. She has signed the picture as a souvenir. It was taken in 1894, two years after the property was taken over by the Birthplace Trust. Note the changes to the gardens and outbuildings that are already giving the house its familiar image.

MRS BAKER died in 1899. Many of the dignitaries at her funeral must have reflected on this severing of a link with a vanishing past. The Revd George Arbuthnot conducts the burial service at Stratford cemetary.

A RARE VIEW OF THE REAR OF THE PROPERTY, taken in 1874, on a fine summer's day. Clearly the two gentlemen in the picture are enjoying the balmy atmosphere. Perhaps they have sampled ale from the barrels by the door of the neighbouring farm-building. After the death of Mrs Baker, the Birthplace Trust turned the Hathaway home into a museum. It must be one of the world's most photographed buildings.

# 'About the Best Beer Brewed in England'

The brewery established by Edward Flower flourished. In 1852 it was rebuilt on three times the scale. Technical innovation – Flower's was the first brewery to introduce coolers – helped produce what Punch described as 'about the best beer brewed in England'.

Over the years Flower's Brewery established a domination of the local trade, although they never achieved a monopoly. For many years the Oddfellows remained Stratford's last home-brew house; it was taken over by Flower's in the 1920s. The owners from the 1850s were a well-known family of licensees, the Eboralls, whose members kept pubs in Stratford for many years.

Many of the pubs pictured here have closed their doors; particularly since Whitbread's closed the brewery in 1968.

THE REBUILT BREWERY, pictured by the *Illustrated Midland News.*

THIS STEAM WAGON made deliveries to the pubs in the latter part of Victoria's reign.

THE FLOWERS WERE PHILANTHROPIC EMPLOYERS, solicitous of their employees' welfare. A brewery club was established and Sarah Flower, daughter-in-law of the brewery's founder, established a school. Strong traditions of working in the brewery were established among local families. This picture of the brewery's coopers was taken around 1879. Note the hoops for putting round the barrels and also the basket of barrel corks held by the man in the middle.

ONE OF THE FIRST PUBS THAT FLOWER'S ACQUIRED was the Stratford Arms in Henley Street (above). It closed in 1912. This picture was taken around 1908, the year in which J.H. Cooper opened his fish and chip shop. Note also the Coach and Horses on the left, another Flower's pub. It closed in the 1960s and is now a restaurant.

A PUB WHICH CLOSED IN RECENT YEARS was the Talbot, in Bull Street. Thomas Deacon, pictured left, became the landlord in the 1880s.

THE PLYMOUTH ARMS IN WOOD STREET, shortly before it was purchased by Flower's in 1896. Extensive stables housed carriages and hire horses, including those used to pull the town's fire-engine. The Garrick (below), pictured in 1855, is one of Stratford's oldest pubs. It was 'restored' in the 1900s and now looks very different.

THE THATCH IS STRATFORD'S LAST THATCHED BUILDING. It was purchased by Flower's from Hunt Edmunds, the Banbury brewer.

STRATFORD'S LAST HOME-BREW HOUSE, the Oddfellows.

EXPANSION OF TIED HOUSES meant expansion of the brewery: some of the workers in the 1890s are pictured above.

NOT ALL THE PUBS WERE CONTROLLED BY FLOWER'S. The Horse and Jockey, pictured above in the 1860s, was eventually bought by Mitchell's and Butler's and rebuilt in grander style. It closed in 1986, when it was demolished.

SUCH WAS THE WEALTH ENGENDERED BY THE BREWING TRADE that Edward Flower (left) was able to build a mansion, The Hill (below), on the Warwick Road in 1855. The family were great hosts there, entertaining a wide variety of people from the literary and political worlds. Edward Flower was cited as a prime example of the Victorian values of enterprise and philanthropy in Samuel Smiles' famous book, *Self Help*.

EDWARD FLOWER'S SONS, Charles (right) and Edgar, were active in the brewery. Charles' wife, Sarah, was active in education and causes such as the abolition of slavery.

CHARLES BOUGHT AVONBANK, an extensive property by the river, in 1860 and rebuilt it (above). The house was demolished in 1950 and the grounds became part of the Theatre Gardens. The orangery, which may be seen on the right of the property, remains.

IN THE SAME YEAR, Charles was instrumental in forming a local rifle corps. 'It is thought necessary to do so throughout England,' wrote Sarah, 'in case of French invasion.' This picture of the corps was taken at The Firs, in Rother Street, in 1867. Note the fields in what is the modern built-up area around Grove Road.

ANOTHER PICTURE OF VOLUNTEER RIFLEMEN, possibly taken in the same location. The picture dates from around 1870. The bearded volunteer in the back row, right, is John Morgan, local stationer and printer and proprietor of a short-lived newspaper, the *Stratford-upon-Avon Chronicle*.

THE PENCHANT OF THE FLOWERS for interesting people, and their strong Liberalism, led to friendship with the rising Radical, Joseph Chamberlain. The two families acted together in *Fair Rosamund*, a play which Charles Flower had written and, in 1858, the Chamberlains attended a lively Christmas party at The Hill, when eighty-six couples danced until 3 a.m.

ANOTHER NOTED LOCAL LIBERAL PATRICIAN was the Flowers' neighbour, Robert Needham Phillips, a founder of the Anti-Corn Law League and a former MP. He is seen on the left in his library with his youngest daughter, Anna Maria, who married Sir George Trevelyan, who became President of the Board of Trade in Gladstone's third ministry. One of their sons was the prominent historian, G.M. Trevelyan, who was born at Welcombe House (below), the Tudor-style mansion which R.N. Phillips built on land which his father, a prominent Northern industrialist, bought in 1846. The house is now a hotel.

MR PHILLIPS' BROTHER, MARK, was another active Liberal campaigner. He became the first MP for Manchester after the Great Reform Act of 1832. Charles Flower, the Phillips and the Trevelyans all split with Gladstone on the issue of Irish Home Rule, but whereas the Welcombe family returned to the Liberal fold, the Flowers became Conservatives.

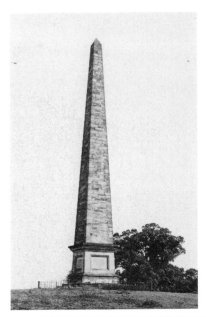

AFTER THE DEATH OF MARK PHILLIPS in 1873, his brother erected this column in his memory, which stands prominently on a hill near Welcombe House.

A PROMINENT LOCAL CONSERVATIVE WAS SIR ANTHONY HODGSON, an affable paternalist who was five times Mayor of Stratford. An old Etonian, he made a fortune sheepfarming in Queensland, where he became Prime Minister. The Hodgsons lived in Clopton House, an ancient mansion just outside the town which was the home of the Clopton family for a long time. The house has associations with the Gunpowder Plot. It was rented by Ambrose Rookwood in 1605 in order that he might be near his fellow conspirators, who were mainly impoverished local gentry.

## SECTION NINE

# 'Everything Conspired to Make the Occasion Happy'

*In 1858, at the annual dinner of the Shakespeare Club, Harries Tilbury, the comic actor, suggested a grand celebration to commemorate the three hundredth anniversary of the birth of William Shakespeare in 1864. A committee was formed under the chairmanship of Edward Flower. There was a strong tradition of such occasions in Stratford, starting with the famous Garrick Jubilee of 1769. Indeed many locals were upset because a lot of the traditional elements like pageants, were absurd. So an alternative festival was organized which included a parade and a circus.*

*The festival was a great success, although it lost money. It proved that thousands of people could be persuaded to visit Stratford for events associated with Shakespeare. This lesson was not lost on Charles Flower.*

EDWARD FLOWER BECAME MAYOR OF STRATFORD for the fourth time in 1863. He was described as 'looking like a Doge of Venice when a Doge was a Doge indeed'. Plans were already afoot to celebrate the tercentenary of the birth of William Shakespeare in the following years. A huge pavilion (above right), modelled on John O'Groat's House, was erected on land owned by Charles Flower in Southern Lane. Note the men, presumably the builders, on the roof.

EDWARD FLOWER'S WIFE, SELINA (left), was originally from Barford. They married in 1827.

A HUGE DINNER was held in the pavilion to open the proceedings.

PERFORMANCES OF SHAKESPEARE'S PLAYS, featuring leading actors of the day, such as Edward Compton (seen here playing Davy Garrick in London, years later), brought huge crowds to Stratford, although some important players refused to appear because they felt that the parts they were playing were not good enough.

THE THEATRE IN CHAPEL LANE — now called The Royal Shakespeare Rooms — had closed its doors for the last time in 1872. Charles Flower resolved to build a grander one on a riverside site and donated the land and much of the money to do so. The Shakespeare Memorial Association opened a public subscription in 1874, to build a theatre complete with library, art gallery and, if possible, Charles Flower's dream of an acting school. After a competition, the design of Dodgshun and Unsworth of Westminster was accepted. The foundation stone was laid on 23 April 1877, Shakespeare's birthday, when five hundred freemasons processed to the site to see the Provincial Grand Master, Lord Leigh, carry out the ceremony with appropriate ritual. The scene is depicted above in what is probably the oldest photograph in existence of a public event in Stratford. Sarah Flower found the gentlemen who spoke at the ceremony nervous, 'except my dear Husband who knew his well, and his delivery was the best of any, short and concise and good.'

ROOFING THE THEATRE, 1878. The turrets and gables are emerging, all faintly reminiscent, in an odd Victorian way, of Shakespeare's Globe.

WORK ON THE NEW THEATRE was hampered by water on the site – the Meer Pool stream ran across it – and by the floods of 1878. Note the warehouse on the Bancroft.

A NEW LANDMARK was being added to the Stratford skyline. The warehouse remains on the Bancroft in the picture above, but gradually the old industrial site was converted to public gardens and the canal basins became ornamental lakes (below).

A CHARMING GLIMPSE of the old Stratford and the new. The osier beds remain by the river, shortly to be replaced by formal gardens; Waterside is a track with a grass verge; one of the last generation of labourers to wear a smock wends his way homewards, and beyond rises the Shakespeare Memorial Theatre. The auditorium is complete, but the water tower has not yet been built. The Black Swan, on the left, was to become a noted theatrical hostelry.

THE THEATRE was completed in 1879. The picture on the left shows the main vestibule. The circle entrance is up the stairs. This is now the entrance to the Swan Theatre.

THE AUDITORIUM, with seating for 800. A section of the stage, the original act drop (painted by local artist, W.W. Quatremain) and the proscenium arch may be seen on the right, with the orchestra pit, complete with music stands, in front.

THE OPENING PRODUCTION on 23 April 1879, Shakespeare's birthday, was *Much Ado About Nothing*. The famous actress, Helen Faucit, was persuaded to come out of retirement to play Beatrice opposite Barry Sullivan's Benedick. Despite having to brave driving rain to attend (traditionally it always rains on great Stratford occasions), a capacity audience demonstrated huge enthusiasm. 'Everything', wrote Helen Faucit, 'conspired to make the occasion happy.'

AT FIRST the London critics were either contemptuous of the new theatre, or they ignored it. The earliest seasons only lasted a week and Stratford seemed far away from the bright lights of the West End. The picture changed in 1882, when the adulated young American actress, Mary Anderson (left), announced her intention to make her debut as Rosalind during the Stratford season. There was a scramble for tickets and every hotel was jammed. To commemorate her performances at Stratford, Miss Anderson donated two terracotta panels depicting Comedy and Tragedy, which stand above the old circle entrance (below).

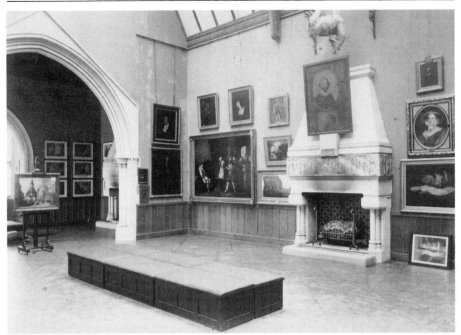

THE THEATRE CONTAINED AN ART GALLERY, which held a fine collection of theatrical pictures.

AN IMPRESSIVE ADDITION to the setting of the theatre came in 1888 when Lord Ronald Gower unveiled his memorial to Shakespeare in the Theatre Gardens. It took twelve years to complete and was executed in Paris. In 1933 it was moved to a site on the Bancroft.

CHARLES FLOWER'S MAYORAL YEAR, 1879, was an important one for Stratford in another way. The outlying villages like Shottery were incorporated into the Borough. Also included was Alveston, a village upstream but then entirely separate. It too had a rural air as is seen by these pictures of the village policeman and a besmocked labourer crossing the river by ferry.

# 'Send me a Good Fast Bowler to Play Laertes'

*It was the actor F.R. Benson, who, more than anyone else, put Stratford into its place in the theatrical firmament. He and his company appeared there in most seasons between their debut in 1886 and 1919. He made his last appearance on the Stratford stage at the opening of the new Shakespeare Memorial Theatre in 1932. As well as producing a generation of actors, the company were noted for their sporting prowess and the Bensonian spirit is well expressed in this section heading – a legendary telegram sent by F.R.B. to his agent.*

CHARLES AND SARAH FLOWER saw the young Frank Benson (left) play Macbeth at Leamington Spa in 1885. As befits the 'Scottish Play', the production was a disaster, but the Flowers had seen the essence of 'good shows' and the Benson Company was engaged to perform the following Stratford season.

BENSON'S FIRST PERFORMANCE AT STRATFORD, as Hamlet (right), won great acclaim: favourable comparisons were made with Henry Irving.

THE ENCHANTMENT WITH BENSON was reciprocated. He wrote to his fiancée, enthusing about the town and the Flowers, who conducted their theatre with 'personal love and reverence'. The stage hands were all locals on a week's secondment. Stratfordians also appeared on stage, and friends in the gallery shouted their names. Benson was delighted by this interplay between theatre and town. Waterside, pictured above, an attractive street where ordinary people lived, was the main approach to the theatre.

FOR PRODUCTIONS OF *A MIDSUMMER NIGHT'S DREAM*, Benson would employ up to fifty local children to play the fairies. In 1899 Benjamin Stone caught some of the girls rehearsing the Fairies' Dance in the Theatre Gardens:

Hand in hand with Fairy Grace
Will we sing and bless this place.

IT WAS IN *A MIDSUMMER NIGHT'S DREAM*, in 1888, that Constance Benson made her Stratford debut. She was a great success, playing it 'all gauze and huge butterfly wings'. Years later she reflected 'I must have spent months of my life on the bank.'

WHEN THE COMPANY ARRIVED for the 1893 season, Benson was suffering from typhoid and was rushed to bed in a delirium. A prominent Bensonian, Lyall Swete, learnt most of the part of Petruchio in a day and improvised the rest. He is seen here in a London performance with George Alexander (left), who also appeared at Stratford several times.

AN ACCOMPLISHED BUT NOT BRILLIANT ACTRESS, whose voice some considered too shrill, Mrs Benson played Katherine in the same production.

A YOUNG AND VERY LARGE AUST-RALIAN, OSCAR ASCHE, later famous in musical comedy, made his debut that season. He is pictured here with his wife, the beautiful actress, Lily Brayton, who also played many Stratford seasons.

EACH SEASON the company performed a new play. Because of Benson's illness, it was decided to bring the company back in August to do *Coriolanus*. This second season became a regular practice and represents the first extension of the programme. The weather was splendidly hot and many of the rehearsals were in the garden of the Black Swan, dubbed by the actors the Dirty Duck, a name which has stuck till this day.

LOCAL MEMORY has exaggerated the extent of Bensonian sporting activity in Stratford: the actors were only there for a comparatively brief period and much of that was taken up with rehearsing and acting. Nevertheless, fixtures were played against local clubs in a number of sports. Benson believed strongly in the value of sport in building an *esprit de corps* among his company. Above is a Bensonian soccer team of the 1890s. Benson is, inevitably, captain. Mrs Benson holds the bouquet. Richmond, Benson's legendary dresser, is the bowler-hatted figure on the right. O.P. Clarence, seated on the ground, centre, survived to play the 'Aged P' in the post-war film of *Great Expectations*. The great bulk of Oscar Asche (centre) filled the goal for the Bensonians at both soccer and hockey (above right).

THE NEW PRODUCTION in 1894 was *Henry IV, Part Two*. Constance Benson's Doll Tearsheet, her finest role, was modelled on a prostitute she had seen in Manchester. Several clergymen preached against it (although none had seen the production). Thirty years later she concluded that Victorian morality considered it 'highly immoral to "make vice attractive".'

PRODUCTIONS AT STRATFORD became more and more elaborate, with great attention paid to detail. The Theatre Orchestra played an important role in this.

THE CELEBRATED FRENCH ACTRESS, Sarah Bernhardt, came to Stratford in 1899, for a special performance of her famed *Hamlet*, in French prose, supported by the Bensonians. Thousands greeted her arrival at the station. She described the visit as 'one of my heart's memories'.

# A New Era

*Another legendary character became associated with Stratford in 1899, when Marie Corelli, the popular novelist, moved to the town. The author of* The Sorrows of Satan, Barabbas *and many other best-sellers was then at the peak of her fame. It was not long before Stratford discovered that her presence was a mixed blessing.*

MARIE CORELLI HATED TO BE PHOTOGRAPHED. This rare picture was taken fifteen years after her arrival in Stratford. She is with her companion, the Belgian aristocrat, Bertha Vyver.

CORELLI RENTED HALL'S CROFT, once the home of Shakespeare's son-in-law, John Hall, a distinguished doctor.

SHE WAS NOT AN EASY NEIGHBOUR. Opposite was the girls' school run by the formidable Mrs Cameron Stuart. Repeated requests from Marie to curb the normal noise of the school were ignored. In a huff, she moved down the street to Avonbank. While there, she entertained the members of the exclusive Whitefriars Club, who included Sir Henry Irving and Winston Churchill.

MARIE MOVED TO MASON'S CROFT in Church Street soon after. The sender of this postcard has written, 'Too peaceful looking an abode for the author of the Sorrows of Satan...'

IT WAS NOT LONG before Marie was at loggerheads with her neighbours, Trinity College. The house next door had long served as the school laundry until it was demolished in 1899.

THE VICTORIAN ERA WAS DRAWING TO A CLOSE. These oxen were part of the procession to mark the Queen's Diamond Jubilee in 1897.

AT THE END OF THE REIGN Britain was at war with the Boers. The Warwickshire Yeomanry served in South Africa. Lieut. Richard Fordham Flower (right), son of Edgar Flower, was killed at Hammond's Kraal.

A NEW REIGN: the Coronation of Edward VII, 1902. The Mayor of Stratford, preceded by his mace-bearers, leads a procession of dignitaries up Church Street on the way to a service of celebration in Holy Trinity Church. In Victoria's sixty-four-year reign, Stratford had been transformed from the town which Shakespeare might have known, to something closer to the place we know today. Further rapid change would come in the twentieth century and not everyone would be sure that it was entirely for the better.